BACK STORY

Based on characters created

by

JOAN ACKERMANN

A dramatic anthology by

Joan Ackermann, Courtney Baron, Neena Beber, Constance Congdon, Jon Klein, Shirley Lauro, Craig Lucas, Eduardo Machado, Donald Margulies, Jane Martin, Susan Miller, John Olive, Tanya Palmer, David Rambo, Edwin Sánchez, Adele Edling Shank, Mayo Simon and Val Smith

* * * *

This play was commissioned by

Actors Theatre of Louisville

Dramatic Publishing

Woodstock, Illinois • England • Australia • New Zealand

*** NOTICE ***

DRAMATIC PUBLISHING
P. O. Box 129, Woodstock, Illinois 60098

Printed in the United States of America

(BACK STORY)

ISBN 1-58342-022-3

IMPORTANT BILLING AND CREDIT REQUIREMENTS

All producers of the play *must* give credit to the authors of the play in all programs distributed in connection with performances of the play and in all instances in which the title of the play appears for purposes of advertising, publicizing or otherwise exploiting the play and/or a production. Credit shall read as follows:

BACK STORY
a dramatic anthology based on characters created by
Joan Ackermann
by
Joan Ackermann, Courtney Baron, Neena Beber,
Constance Congdon, Jon Klein, Shirley Lauro,
Craig Lucas, Eduardo Machado, Donald Margulies,
Jane Martin, Susan Miller, John Olive, Tanya Palmer,
David Rambo, Edwin Sánchez, Adele Edling Shank,
Mayo Simon and Val Smith.

The names of the authors *must* appear in size of type not less than fifty percent the size of the title type.

On all programs this notice should appear:

"Produced by special arrangement with
THE DRAMATIC PUBLISHING COMPANY of Woodstock, Illinois"

All producers of the play must include the following acknowledgment on the title page of all programs distributed in connection with performances of the play and on all advertising and promotional materials:

"This piece was originally commissioned by
Actors Theatre of Louisville."

BACK STORY

A two-character play in 19 scenes and monologues.
Can be played with any combination of male and female actors, from 1m and 1w to 11m and 11w.

Contents

Humana Festival Production

Back Story was commissioned by Actors Theatre of Louisville and premiered at the Humana Festival of New American Plays in March 2000. It was directed by Pascaline Bellegarde, Aimée Hayes, Dano Madden, Meredith McDonough and Sullivan Canaday White with the following cast:

ETHAN . . . . Phil Bolin, Cary Calebs, Patrick Dall'Occhio, Jeff Jenkins, Tom Johnson, Cabe McCarty, Tom Moglia, Stephen Sislen, Mark Watson, Zach Welsheimer, Travis York

AINSLEY . . . . . . Shawna Joy Anderson, Molly M. Binder, Rachel Burttram, Christy Collier, Samantha Desz, Melody G. Fenster, Aimée Kleisner, Kimberly Megna, Holly W. Sims, Heather Springsteen, Jessica Wortham

and the following production staff:

Scenic Designer . . . . Paul Owen
Costume Designer. . . . . Kevin McLeod
Lighting Designer . . . . Greg Sullivan
Sound Designers . . Darron L. West and Martin R. Desjardins
Properties Designer. . . . . Mark Walston
Stage Manager . . . . Amber D. Martin
Dramaturgs . . . Michael Bigelow Dixon and Amy Wegener
Assistant Dramaturg . . . . Kerry Mulvaney

The Making of *Back Story*

by Amy Wegener and Michael Bigelow Dixon, Dramaturgs, Actors Theatre of Louisville

"What's the character's back story?" This question is a familiar one for actors working to build a psychologically complex role out of the clues provided in a dramatic text. By imagining the character's past, or what has happened outside of the immediate action represented in the play, the actor strives to find ways of informing, deepening, and rendering immediate the moments revealed onstage.

But consider what could happen to the way we think about creating characters if this process were reversed: what if a richly detailed character history—or the intertwined histories of two characters, say a brother and sister in their early twenties—became the imaginative impetus for not just one, but a multitude of playwrights and their texts? And what if these varied perspectives could come together to make one theatrical event?

These questions are at the heart of the challenge embraced by *Back Story*, an experiment based on a tale penned by Joan Ackermann. Ackermann's wonderfully textured and suggestive story details the adventures and misadventures of Ainsley and Ethan Belcher of Pittsfield, Massachusetts, siblings whose close relationship evolves throughout their lifetimes and reaches a pivotal moment in the year 2000. Using this narrative as a springboard, Ackermann and seventeen other talented dramatists wrote three scenes and sixteen monologues for Ainsley and Ethan. For the Humana Festival premiere of *Back Story*, the siblings were portrayed by eleven men and eleven women in Actors Theatre's 1999-2000 Apprentice Acting Company (though they could be played by as few as two actors). The spirit of collaboration inherent in the project extended to the direction of the festival production as well: *Back Story* was staged by five directors, working together to discover the larger portrait created by so many authorial (and actors') voices and styles.

This collaborative process began with the creation of the text, which required some logistical planning in order to build upon the rich foundation provided by Joan Ackermann's story. In addition to this narrative, Ackermann had been commissioned to write the first monologue and last scene of the play, which provided "bookends" for the other pieces. The rest of the playwrights, who had agreed to write either a two-minute monologue or a six-minute scene, received copies of the story, and were invited to contact us with several "moments" in the narrative that they would be interested in exploring. Over the course of several weeks, we spoke with each writer about these choices and their ideas, and coordinated their selections so that we could "cover" as much of the back story as possible, encouraging variety while also ensuring some sense of progression through time and events for both Ethan and Ainsley.

In general, we hypothesized that successful pieces would expand upon a "moment" in the story in some depth, rather than simply relating information from the story. There were a few basic guidelines as well: 1) The details of a piece could not contradict details in the story, 2) Moments from the past had to be explored actively in the present, since actors in their twenties could not plausibly play children or young teenagers, and 3) There could not be too many pieces using the same modes of address (writing a letter, for example). The playwrights generously shared their own questions and ideas about the process with us, which helped us to address many complications early on. Once everyone had "dibs" on a chunk of the story, they set out to compose their pieces.

When the first drafts began to pour into the literary office, we were delighted to discover that there was great variety in the work—the pieces ranged from outrageously funny to lyrical to philosophical in tone, and were as different as the actors who would eventually perform them. But already, a thematic coherence began to emerge. Certain images or ideas became motifs in several pieces, and the authors had developed some of the major currents in Ethan and Ainsley's relationship: the loss of a father who goes on a fishing trip to Alaska and never returns, Ainsley's self-sacrifice in her devotion to Ethan and her relationship with music, Ethan's entrepreneurial spirit and "uncontrolled velocity." Of course, there were some rewrites and cuts to coordinate and small contradictions to iron out, and many of the pieces continued to be refined throughout the rehearsal process. But somehow, in pursuing their own passions in depth, the playwrights had been able to hop onto the same wavelength while remaining wildly diverse.

The next step was to ponder how we could thread together these individual parts to shape the whole event. So we began an ongoing discussion about the order of the scenes and monologues: What kind of trajectory were the characters following together? What were Ethan's and Ainsley's individual "arcs" through the event? In what ways would chronology be important? How would some pieces set up information that would inform others? How could we vary the energy and tone of the work while building a set of impressions that would create a story?

Rehearsals began at odd hours and in odd corners of the building, with a weekly read-through (and later, run-throughs) so that everyone could chart *Back Story*'s progress. We heard several running orders for the pieces, settling on the performance order you see in this volume after much discussion and debate. The directors worked on transitions in order to make the show as seamless as possible, and fruitful questions continued to sharpen our collective sense of the characters, both as individual constructs and in relationship with each other. Many minds continued to strive to create a unified experience.

When audiences came to see the five performances scheduled during the Humana Festival, they were faced with a choice which would impact their experience: to read Ackermann's story beforehand, or to see the play without the benefit of having already digested the narrative upon which its many parts are based. We don't know which is the preferable choice, but we think that they deliver different kinds of pleasures. On the one hand, reading the story allows one to see how it has been adapted and to appreciate the authors' varying approaches; on the other, seeing the performance without this preparation allows an encounter with the characters which (we think) holds together on its own terms. In other words, if the back story is a colorful, high-resolution map of these characters' lives, then the play *Back Story* travels through an exploration of "stops," impressions, and turning points in their journey.

* * * *

BACK STORY
the story by Joan Ackermann

Part I

When Ethan Belcher was nearly born during a blizzard at three in the morning in the back of his father's van en route to Hillcrest Hospital in Pittsfield, Mass., his sister Ainsley chopped her toe off with a snow shovel on their front porch. She was two and a half years old, barefoot in six inches of soft snow, clad only in a motley-colored, hand-crocheted jersey with an unfinished right arm. Left in the care of her great-aunt Lou, who collapsed to sleep on the broken recliner after all the drama with the jumper cables and the van had fishtailed out the driveway, Ainsley had bolted out the front door.

She could hear Lou's fitful snoring as she stood perched on the top of eight steps. The strangled sounds of tortured breathing almost supported her tiny frame as she swayed in the cold night air, blinking at updrafts of snow in the lights from the street lamps, the tears on her face slowly freezing over. Ainsley had screamed, howled with wild blue-faced uncharacteristic force to be taken to the hospital with her parents. "It's the baby," Lou had cooed, following the toddler around, attempting to calm her hysteria as Gloria and Jim hunted desperately for a flashlight. "It's all right, sweetie. The baby is coming." But Lou was only throwing fuel on the flames. Ainsley's awareness that the baby was coming was keener than anyone's in the family, including her mother Gloria, who was now cursing her husband as he ruefully tried to dig the van out of a snowdrift.

If Ainsley had been aware that the brown van which bore the chipped letters "Belcher Electric" had skidded off the road at the bottom of the hill, she might have jumped from the lip of the porch down into the night to rescue her baby brother. As it was, Reuben, their sixty-year-old tenant, discovered Ainsley crouched on the porch with the five-foot shovel, when he staggered home from a late night of drinking. He had the presence of mind to find her toe, frozen and preserved in the snow. Reuben was the only one in that household to realize that Ainsley's accident with the snow shovel was a mission derailed. He alone saw her intention had been to clear the way for the baby's arrival.

And so it was that Ainsley Belcher arrived at the hospital after all, in time to be there for her younger brother. As the last stitch was sewn into place on her tiny foot, a barely coherent Reuben holding her hand, she heard Ethan's first cries from down the hall. It was not the last time she would sacrifice some part of her self in his behalf. Nor was it the last time that he would arrive late, that his movement would unleash havoc and drama, and that he would be unaware of his sister's efforts.

They all stayed in the hospital that night, the bad weather preventing travel. Long after Gloria, Jim and Reuben had escaped their disjointed lives in deep slumber, Ainsley remained awake on a cot in the hall, listening for every sound from the baby. As Ethan blindly waved tiny punches in the air, his body involuntarily twitched in her direction, turned by the sound of her small voice, singing to him.

Part II

In the summer of '81, Jim Belcher took off for a two-week fishing trip in Alaska. Ainsley was seven and Ethan was five. Gloria had just been promoted to dining room manager at Captain Toss's seafood restaurant and was in unusually good spirits, frosting her hair and buying short suits at Filene's Basement at the Holyoke Mall. Even at home her gait had a gyrating spring to it, as if her backside were still the viewing target of a counter full of lunching tradesmen. She cheerfully helped Jim pack for his lifelong dream trip. Bought him a quilted reversible jacket. Hand warmers. When the family loaded him and his poles onto the Bonanza bus for New York City, not even Jim, embarrassed by unexpected tears, had an inkling he wasn't coming back.

Reuben, the Belchers' tenant, introduced Ainsley to the clarinet that summer. For thirty years he had played with the Boston Symphony Orchestra before a complete physical and mental breakdown had broken him permanently. She would lay the instrument flat on his bed with the mouthpiece hanging over the edge and toot into it, standing, playing an open G while he sat in an unraveling rattan chair and mumbled encouragement. Outside, Ethan would throw up gravel. Every now and then a small white piece would sail through the open window and Ainsley would go down to keep him company.

Like a goat, Ethan had eradicated any sign of greenery in the fenced-in yard. Possessed of a mind that was a train yard of derailing and colliding engines, his body had its own uncontrolled velocity. His ability to effect total change on his surroundings in seconds was noteworthy for one so small. At five, he was forbidden from the local supermarket. An electrician's son, he aimed for current, plugging in and turning on anything that bore a cord. The Doberman next door lost all control of its bladder when in view of the towheaded boy. Only Ainsley could contain and calm her brother. Her love for him was predicated on a need so great, she was not to be budged from it. She forgave him for putting her hamster in the freezer. (He said he thought it would hibernate.) For washing all her stickers in the bathtub.

By the fall of '81, Gloria's bright spirits had dimmed, her backside uncoiled. She was working twelve-hour days and had exchanged her high heels for sneakers. Jim's last card, a picture of disoriented caribou grouped by the pipeline, offered one sentence expressing a need for time to think. She was rarely home and when she was, she slept. The household subsisted on a steady seafood diet from the restaurant—coquilles St. Jacques for breakfast, clam chowder for snack. great-aunt Lou did the housekeeping, moving with the Hoover slowly, steadily, from room to room and floor to floor like a sea snail in an aquarium, sucking up debris.

The day before he was to enter kindergarten, Ethan disappeared. Ainsley found him after midnight buried in the back of the cake room. A professional cake decorator, great-aunt Lou had saved every cake that hadn't sold or been picked up. The sewing room on the third floor had become storage for hundreds of cakes in white boxes, some as old as thirty years, sculptures of hardened wedding cakes, Fourth of July cakes, ornate icing designs now rigid as set plaster. After Ainsley had helped Ethan crawl out, she tucked him into bed with the three clam shells he had guarded from dinner the day before.

It was chilly that night. A frost was predicted. She closed the window down hard on the rake rigged out the window with a twenty-foot piece of string tied at the tip. "I'm fishing for daddy!!" Ethan would wail at Gloria every time she tried to take it down. Cold wind ripped through the room in the crack past the rake handle, as Ainsley burrowed deep in her bed. She pictured her father on an ice floe, with a polar bear, surrounded by time to think. Ethan's eyes were closed and twitching. His fearful dread of his imminent academic career was in fact wholly justified, in actuality not an unadmirable indication of self-knowledge and awareness of his own limitations.

Part III

By the time Ethan dropped out of high school the day he turned sixteen, he had four business cards—one for a lawn mowing business, a bicycle messenger service, a VCR and television repair service, and a "Pittsfield, the Heart of the Berkshires" information hot line. Pittsfield was more the liver of the Berkshires with the General Electric plant pumping the bile, and Ethan rarely received calls on his hot line, but his other endeavors turned over handy profits. His sixteenth year he made more money than his mother who now worked the night shift at

Dunkin Donuts. The used scuba diving gear he'd invested in to retrieve golf balls from a pond across from the golf course had been paid off twice over just from the sale of the balls. (Though he'd nearly drowned on a moonless night when his tank was empty and he was full of beer, unable to tell which way was up. His friend Willis hauled him out.)

He went through a tour-guiding period, bicycling fifteen miles down to Stockbridge to give tours at the Norman Rockwell Museum (Gloria used to take her children there after Jim left, feeling both comforted and shattered by the heartwarming scenes of domestic normalcy); to Glendale, to guide visitors at Chesterwood, home of sculptor Daniel French (he was seduced by a trustee in French's studio who later accused him of chipping the plaster model of the Lincoln Memorial when in fact she had flailed it over); and to Pittsfield's own Arrowhead, home of Herman Melville. Ethan had a gift for memorizing large chunks of text which proved useful because he was never able to learn to read well. Ainsley, who had read him thousands of pages since childhood, read him all the literature of these establishments, and he repeated it verbatim with a great charm and grin that endeared him to vacationing New Yorkers. He enhanced his tours with wildly creative and interesting lies.

When he was fired from Arrowhead for adamantly arguing against the in-house speculation that it was the distant rounded form of Mt. Greylock, seen from the second-story window, that had inspired Melville to write a book about a whale there ("Oh, and the fact that he had been on several whaling expeditions had *nothing* to do with his choice of subject?"), he gave up tour-guiding. The money wasn't that great, and Willis had stopped trying to commit suicide and was now fooling around with computers. They joined forces.

Whereas Ethan's energies were manic and outwardly directed, Ainsley's were ingrown and unprofitable. As an adolescent, she drifted in a perpetual haze of longing, finding some release in her journal, the occasional poem. She was an unremarkable student, slipping by her teachers unnoticed, aiming primarily for invisibility. Only when defending her brother did her will surge to the forefront. At fourteen, she railed at the teacher who had scrawled the word "moron" on one of his rare attempts at writing. In a jailhouse in Danville, New Hampshire, she gave the cop such a headache he let Ethan out of his cell. (He'd been arrested for hitchhiking and drinking under age. She'd borrowed Reuben's car to drive up and retrieve him.) She went to the house of the thirteen-year-old kid who was supplying Ethan with pot and acid, and smacked him out of that inclination. Only once did she have a major run-in with her mother, over something inconsequential. It was a token gesture of rage; for the most part, her mother was too deflated to engage in battle. Her sad face already declared, "I have lost."

Throughout her childhood and adolescence, Reuben occasionally took Ainsley to Saturday morning rehearsals at Tanglewood, summer home of the Boston Symphony Orchestra. Several of the musicians remembered Reuben, he'd been first clarinetist, including visiting conductor Leonard Bernstein who kissed the back of Ainsley's hand. Bernstein was her first love; tanned, aged, Byronic. She sat, eleven years old, transfixed—pigeons cooing above in the open-aired shed—and stared at his impassioned conducting, his expressive hands, his long white hair. At home, she practiced the clarinet, shut up in the cake room, imagining him conducting her in Beethoven's "Ode to Joy."

In high school, Ainsley joined the track team and was startled to break a short distance record in her first meet. But she preferred long distance, running the old logging roads up October Mountain, the smell of wet, decaying leaves underfoot, the descent in the dark as the days grew shorter. She eventually quit the team because everyone pressed her to compete and she really didn't want to. Her best friend Helena (whose parents owned Sophia's, a Greek restaurant where Ainsley bussed tables) talked her into joining the school band. Ainsley's bruising crush on the unattainable Mr. Harnette, the music teacher whose witty sarcasm took her breath away, caused far more pain than pleasure. Her junior year, after Helena had graduated and gone off to

Smith College, he encouraged Ainsley to take up the oboe. It was a life-changing event. The instrument—which Mr. Harnette rented for her with his own money (the band lacked an oboist and funds)—answered her soul's cry for reciprocity. She gave it her breath and it responded; spoke back to her in plaintive harrowing notes. Mossy night sounds from deep moonlit forests. It was harder to play than the clarinet, the reed more complex and strange. She'd stare at it by candlelight as it soaked upside down in a glass of water.

She practiced night and day, playing woodwind duets with Reuben, who was gaining weight from all the boxes of Dunkin Donuts. The old Doberman next door (who had survived being run over by Ethan's Suburban; he'd apologized to the Grundys), hid in the basement from the unbearable strains. Ainsley composed her own music, traveled boldly and instinctively into uncharted territory. Her new-found voice brought her ashore. By the time she was nineteen, her haze had lifted. Her force field repolarized, she became visible, attractive; acquired sardonic wit. She was accepted at the Boston Conservatory of Music (Mr. Harnette, who, unbeknownst to Ainsley, was deeply in love with her, arranged the audition), but she declined their offer of admission.

In the spring of her senior year, she lost her virginity to an Appalachian Trail thru-hiker who lost his heart to her and wanted to quit the trail, but she levelheadedly convinced him to continue. She'd picked him up hitchhiking into town to buy groceries and he'd hung around for a month. After he left, every few weeks she'd send a package of chocolate and Little Debbies to the next P.O. on the list he'd given her of post offices that dotted his route down to Springer Mountain. She addressed the packages to his trail name, Mango Madness.

After high school, she worked first at General Electric, then at Grossman's Lumber, then at Canyon Ranch, a forty-million-dollar health spa where, as a program coordinator, she set up individual programs for guests (including Barbra Streisand who changed her massage appointment every ten seconds), and then back at Grossman's Lumber where she dated the yard foreman. At home, great-aunt Lou was bedridden, but Reuben, now eighty-three and recharged by playing duets with Ainsley, joined the community orchestra and was making an effort to comb his hair and to remember to wear his dentures. Gloria was running her own video store, set up in business by Ethan, who was making excellent money installing and servicing computers with Willis.

On Thanksgiving morning in the year 2000, Ethan told Ainsley that his eighteen-year-old girlfriend Kimmy was pregnant and asked her what they should do. Ainsley said that Kimmy should move in with them and have the baby there. Gloria, after her initial shock, grimaced but then warmed to the idea. That evening, with great-aunt Lou halfheartedly protesting from the second floor, the three of them cleared out the cake room to be the baby's room. They pitched the white boxes out the window and swept the oak floor, exposed for the first time in nearly fifty years. Later, after everyone had gone to bed—Reuben, with bad indigestion from the creamed onions—Ainsley and Ethan sat down at the kitchen table and wrote their father Jim a letter, advising him he was going to be a grandfather and sending congratulations.

* * * *

BACK STORY

Time to Think

Joan Ackermann

(AINSLEY, age eighteen, enters, wearing an unbuttoned winter coat, sorrel snow boots, a scarf around her neck.)

AINSLEY. August twentieth, the summer I was seven, my dad was supposed to come home from a fishing trip in Alaska. He didn't. Some time around the middle of September we got a postcard from him saying he needed time to think. That was all he wrote. "I need time to think."

(Yelling upstairs.) Ethan! We're leaving in two minutes!

My mother was in no mood to explain what his message meant, and I couldn't figure it out. "Time to think." When I was seven, all I *had* was time. If only I could have given some to my dad. The fact that he never came home created a whole lot of more time. Time to miss him. Time to try to figure out why he couldn't just come back and think in Pittsfield, Mass.

(Yelling up.) I'm not kidding! Ethan!

(She does the buttons up on her coat and whips her scarf around.)

I wondered, was there a particular quality to time in Alaska that made him need to do his thinking there? I knew he was in a *different* time. My mother said we couldn't call him first thing in the morning because he'd still be asleep. That in itself was weird. Being an electrician, he was always up hours before the rest of us, at the crack of dawn, fooling with his tools in the back of his van. Belcher Electric. It was disconcerting, actually, to wake up and know he was still asleep. The problem was we were always ahead of him, at any point in the day. In some ways that made us older than him. Less protected.

(She takes a wool hat out of a pocket. Pulls it on. Takes out mittens and puts them on. Glances upstairs.)

The postcard was a picture of a bunch of depressed caribou hanging out by the pipeline in winter. My little brother thought they were Santa's reindeer. I knew they were not. Santa's reindeer were happier. Santa's reindeer were going places. These caribou weren't going anywhere. I taped them up over my bed. I wondered why he'd picked this particular picture for his message. Was he there, with those caribou? Was he planning to stay with them, and think? The key question was, was he thinking about us? Was he thinking about me? *(Pause.)* If he'd chosen a different card it would have been better. And maybe he was wildly happy.

(Yelling up.) Okay I'm leaving! Bye! *(Pause.)* You're walking! Enjoy the freezing rain! *(Pause.)*

People always say, oh how sad, you grew up without a father, your dad left you. It's really not so bad. I don't hold it against him, I really don't. He did what he had to do. And I admire him for that. Probably, at first, he did need time to think. Time to figure out he didn't want to come back. *(Pause.)* Honestly ... ? I don't think about him anymore. I don't have the time. *(Pause.)*

(She doesn't move. Waits for him, all bundled up, still thinking ...)

Good Morning to the Horse

Craig Lucas

(AINSLEY and ETHAN.)

AINSLEY *(reading from a brochure).* "—the view out his bedroom window was like seeing 'out of a porthole of a ship in the Atlantic.' His study he described as his 'ship's cabin,' and when the wind woke him at night he imagined 'there was too much sail on the house.' "... *(Looks up to ETHAN.)* ...Shall I read it again?

ETHAN *(headshake: No).* Mm-mm.

AINSLEY. You have it memorized.

ETHAN *(a nod: Yes).* Mm-hm.

AINSLEY. You do not!

ETHAN *(quickly, no effort).* "Melville claimed that the countryside itself had 'a sort of sea-feeling'... in a letter to his friend Evert Duyckinck, Melville said the view out his bedroom window was like seeing 'out of a porthole of a ship in the Atlantic.' His study he described as his 'ship's cabin,' and when the wind woke him at night he imagined 'there was too much sail on the house.' "

AINSLEY. How do you do that? ...Sooooooo what did he compare his study to?

ETHAN *(quickly murmuring through the spiel once more to find the answer, nearly inaudible except for the end).* "His study he described as his—'ship's cabin' "!!

AINSLEY. Amazing. Okay, go back, how much did he pay for the house?

ETHAN. Heeee— *(Remembers something.)* Oh. Oh. Wait. There's, here in the index, a bunch of references to the house. *(ETHAN retrieves an enormous book.)*

AINSLEY. *Herman Melville!* Did you, what, borrow this?

ETHAN. I bought it.

AINSLEY. Have you ever even bought a book before?

ETHAN. Here's a letter where he describes his working day, after he moves into the house, read this, I can surprise them with this information. During the tour.

AINSLEY. Well, I don't think they expect new guides to be able to rattle off whole letters by Melville.

ETHAN. It refers to the house.

AINSLEY. Even so. Wouldn't it be better to just read the book and call upon the general flavor of things?

ETHAN. Read.

AINSLEY. Why don't you like to read? I love it. *(A little pause, starts to read.)* "Do you want to know how I pass my time? —I rise at—"

ETHAN. You know why? I mean, what. I know what I don't like about reading.

AINSLEY. What?

ETHAN. That it makes things seem like they have a shape.

AINSLEY. What do you mean?

ETHAN. Like things are actually building up to certain events and then other things happen as a result of that annnnd...

AINSLEY. But they do.

ETHAN. Yeah, but it doesn't feel that way when it's happening, it only has a shape when you look back over it or retell it and by then it's too late.

AINSLEY. Too late...?

ETHAN. To do anything, it's already written in stone. When you would need the book is before it happened, not after. What's the big deal, somebody spent their life studying about Herman Melville, everybody knows he's great now, but if somebody could have seen that then they could have recorded a whole helluva lot more about what was going on, and it would have helped Herman to know that he was going to write a great book and people would someday appreciate it.

AINSLEY. Maybe not. Maybe he needed not to know. Or maybe he knew. *(ETHAN shakes his head.)* You don't know.

ETHAN. It's always a lie, 'cause life doesn't feel like it has a shape, life feels like it has no shape, like its only shape and purpose is to foil and scare you and muddle—but books, in books it's like—Life, okay, I mean, Life is like, "Oh no! the car doesn't start. What do I do? Ugh, it's too long to walk, it's raining, I guess I have to bike to Arrowhead for my first day on my new job which I really need." Then: "Oh no! somebody splashed mud on my new suit while I was bicycling. Oh no! they're probably gonna fire me, I hope they don't, maybe I shouuu-uuuuld quick run into the bathroom even though I'm a little bit late and wash this mud off, should I? Shouldn't I? I have no idea, I don't know the end, if I had the book! but okay, I think I will." And then you get it all out, no mudstains, hooray!!! And they fire you for being late, so you SHOULDN'T have washed the mud out, it was time they were worried about, of course not mud, time...

AINSLEY. Everyone's always worried about time. *(Little pause.)* Are you worried they're going to fire you your first day?

ETHAN. And then you get home and oh no! another gas bill. I FORGOT about the gas bill!

AINSLEY *(sniffing)*. Speaking of...

ETHAN. Sorry. *(She swats him.)* The book about all that, describing the rain and the deep, sensual, life-be-deepening color of the mud—

AINSLEY. Be-deepening?

ETHAN *(over her)*. —and the pounding heart and the sinking spirit when the bill, GAS bill, get it!?! the symbolism, gas, it's worthless! AND all books are about bad things happening to people, there are no books in which good and kind people meet and fall in love and raise healthy and respectful and talented and hardworking children and everyone lives into old age.... If a book isn't going to help you with the here and now and it is going to be all that work.... Read.

AINSLEY. You want them all to be happy?... *(Reading.)* "Do you want to know how I pass my time? —I rise at eight—thereabouts—& go to my barn—say good-morning to the horse, & give him his breakfast. (It goes to my heart to give him a cold one, but it can't be helped.) Then, pay a visit to my cow—cut up a pumpkin or two for her, & stand by to see her eat it—for it's a pleasant sight to see a cow move her jaws—she does it so mildly & with such a sanctity. My breakfast over, I—" *(Stops.)* What?

ETHAN. He wrote that!

AINSLEY. I know.

ETHAN. No. He was worried about giving the horse cold food, and he died thinking *Moby Dick* was a failure. Penniless. Completely forgotten.

AINSLEY. How do you—? Did you study it in high school?

ETHAN. It's in, right in there.

AINSLEY. You read this ... whole book?

ETHAN *(over slightly)*. Bits. The end.

AINSLEY. You just read the end?

ETHAN. I always do that.

AINSLEY. Why?

ETHAN. I-I-I-I-I *(Note: the word "I" is drawn out as he debates whether or not he wants to reveal this about himself)* check it first before I start to ... you know ... care about the characters so it won't break my heart when it comes around at the end. If it's ... Go on.

AINSLEY *(resumes reading)*. "I go to my workroom & light my fire—then spread my manuscript on the table—take one business squint at it & fall to with a will. At two and a half P.M. I hear a preconcerted knock at my door, which serves to wean me effectively from my writing, however interested I may be ... My evenings I spend in a sort of a mesmeric state in my room—not being able to read—only now & then skimming some large printed book." *(Pause.)*

ETHAN. Books. *(Pause.)* You see? *(Stands abruptly, wipes his eye as if something got caught in it as he walks out.)* I gotta pee. *(Silence.)*

What Became of the Polar Bear?

Mayo Simon

ETHAN *(offstage)*. ...If you'll all just come this way. Watch your step, please.

(ETHAN enters, speaking in his "tour" voice, with an imaginary tour group.)

ETHAN. In the summer of 1850, Herman Melville, seeking a quiet place to work, bought this 18th-century farmhouse in the town of Pittsfield which was then home to such famous literary figures as Fanny Kemble, Oliver Wendell Holmes, James Russell Lowell, and in Lenox, less than six miles away, Nathaniel Hawthorne. I can repeat that in German. Spanish? French? Serbo-Croatian? Okay, everybody into Herman's study. If you look out the window you can see—Mount Greylock! You'll notice the top of the mountain is shaped like the head of a huge whale. This is the view, ladies and gentlemen, that became the inspiration for Melville's greatest novel, *Moby-Dick*!

(Quietly.) If you believe that, you'll believe anything. Now, you want to hear the real story of how Melville got the idea for *Moby-Dick*?

(Motions people to gather around him.) They don't like me to talk about this—too controversial. But you've been such a good group...

(Looks around, then continues.) Herman Melville was a harpooner on a whaling ship for two years. Started in the South Seas, ended up in the Gulf of Alaska. One foggy morning as the ship is maneuvering around the ice floes where the whales hang out, Melville spies what's left of a fishing boat. Whales get a kick out of ramming boats, so Herman's on the lookout. Sure enough, coming out of the fog, he sees something. It's not a whale. It's...a man...on an ice floe...fishing. Name's Belcher—same name as mine—common name. And on that floe is also...a polar bear. Melville hails the man: "Avast, have you seen a great white whale?" They look at each other, Melville the harpooner, and Belcher, owner and manager of Belcher Electric. Then, as though he's come to some secret and profound conclusion about life, the man raises his arms and...takes off! Actually, a huge whale has crashed up from under the ice, lifting him high in the air. Melville watches as the whale with a giant splash flops down in the water. The man flops down on the whale's back. The whale, with Belcher on his back, dives into the fog and disappears. Awesome. Melville is too stunned to throw the harpoon. Instead, he decides to write a book. It's all in one of Melville's letters to Hawthorne. You can look it up. What's that? What became of the polar bear? Strange you should ask because I ask the same question every night.... What became of him?... That concludes the tour. The gift shop is down the steps and to the right.

The Reluctant Instrument

Neena Beber

AINSLEY. I learned how to kiss on the clarinet ... but I learned how to love on the oboe.

(AINSLEY takes out an oboe and blows into it. Nothing, no sound.)

Unrequited love, my specialty.

Mr. Harnette wants me to play the oboe, I don't know why. Mr. Harnette wants to torture me. The oboe is a complex, difficult instrument. It requires the smallest of breaths. Too much, and the sound is an embarrassment: over-eager and desperate. The oboe requires passion, but also control. Force, but also delicacy.

Mr. Harnette knows: the oboe is the perfect instrument for one doing her best to disappear. When I play, I make myself small and contained. I try to become invisible, to hide inside the sounds as if they belong to someone else.

(Again AINSLEY starts to play, but changes her mind.) I don't think I'll ever get it right.

Mr. Harnette makes music. Mr. Harnette has gray eyes and black hair and wears crisp white shirts. He is a black-and-white photo, a postcard from Paris, a 19th-century novel. He looks best against the snow. He looks best against the snow and that's how I imagine him—have I admitted to imagining him? Gray eyes and black hair and music, music in his soul as I have in mine though he wouldn't know it.

(She tries to play again. A sputter. She sighs, preparing to try again.)

When you play the oboe, you must plan your breathing. You have to decide where to inhale, and where to let go.

(She takes a deep breath.)

The problem is, each time I take a breath I think—I am in love with Mr. Harnette!—and I nearly burst.

In the future I will discover three things, in the following order:

I was a better oboe player than I thought.
The oboe was rented for me not with school band funds, but by Mr. Harnette himself.
My love for Mr. Harnette was not unrequited.

Or maybe I already know that.

Maybe I'll write him a letter. I probably won't. The truth is I definitely won't but there he is—Mr. Harnette—his shades of gray against the snow, someone to return to in a circular breath that comes every so often as breath should.

Full expansive not taking in more than it can give back
A breath that is just right, just enough to set loose
A note
Into the world as I went then
A song waiting to release itself
Steady Clear and
Free.

(AINSLEY plays the oboe. The sound of a solo oboe, culminating in one long, sustaining note.)

Ethan's Got Get

Edwin Sánchez

(ETHAN, wet, and drying his hair, sits by a lake. He takes a swig from a beer bottle. Next to him is a pail of golf balls. He calls out to his friend who is in the lake.)

ETHAN. No, Willis, the other side.

(He points.) I already looked where you are. Now we're looking for a golf ball with a blue stripe around it. That's Mr. Allen's favorite. He'll pay me extra for that one. "Sentimental value."

(Snorts.) Old fool.

(Drinks again and holds up the pail.) Hey look, Willis, I got the town by the balls! Hell, I already paid off the scuba gear twice over just by selling their golf balls back to these guys. Guess when you're old your balls mean a lot to you. Hell, they're old enough. Youngest golfer here is forty if he's a day. They got so much free time, spend their days swinging a club at a little ball. Already made their money, they're set. Not me. But I'm gonna be a millionaire before I'm twenty-one, you watch. Okay, so this is small fry stuff, chump change, but it's a start. This and the other three businesses I got going is

gonna take me up and out. You find Mr. Allen's ball tonight and I'll think about taking you with me.

(Waves to Willis and watches him disappear under water.) No, I won't. Won't take anybody. Just be rich and alone. Finally.

(Picks up one of the balls from the bucket.) Now, how is something like this supposed to have sentimental value? A person, a person who leaves, now that has sentimental value. I mean, I can't go into a sporting goods' store and buy a new father, right? Or buy back my mother's life so she's not tired all the time. Or get Ainsley one of her own so she ain't always trying to share mine. She's just like mama, a born loser.

(To Willis.) You find anything? Well, haul yourself outta there. I got VCRs to fix.

(To himself.) Gotta be successful. Papa left 'cause he couldn't do it. I can. I will.

(Studies one of the balls.) I got a couple of blue Magic Markers at home. Yep, looks like I found your ball, Mr. Allen.

Trying to Get There

Eduardo Machado

AINSLEY. No. Ma, I won't pick up Ethan's dirty dishes and wash them for you. No, I'm sorry, Ma, I won't! *(She looks at her mother.)* No, stay right there. I swear you won't pick them up either. I swear you won't! I demand you won't! No!

Why do I always have to fix everything for him, Ma? Dad left me, too, sure I was older, but Dad left me, too. Why do I always have to take care of everybody? I'm afraid that my entire life will be spent taking care of guys. You know it's the only thing that makes me feel worth something, that and playing music... Do you worry about me, about my future, huh? Ma, don't look away, Ma! Please don't look away. I don't hate him. From the minute he was born...I had to take care of myself. From the night he was born. And I have a missing toe to prove it. If it wasn't for Reuben, I wouldn't have anything, not even music. What am I inheriting, Ma?

Except for silence. Except for being a good girl and keeping my mouth shut. What will I inherit from you, Ma? Except for longing for a man that is never going to come back. My inheritance scares me, Ma. When I look at you I get scared. What will I become, Ma? Speak. Let me hear your opinions. I want to know what you think. Please talk to me. Don't turn on the TV. Please, Ma. Please. No, I don't want to watch that show. 'Cause it's silly, Ma. I think TV is silly.

(She takes a dish. Smashes it against the floor.) I guess nothing will ever make you scream, Ma. I'm going to read. Tell Ethan to sweep the floor.

Maid of Athens

David Rambo

(AINSLEY, nineteen, screams offstage with a startled burst of pain.)

AINSLEY. Shit! Oh ... shit!

(She runs in wrapping a finger in a bloody swath of paper towel. It really hurts. She calls off:)

I'm okay. I've got an ice cube on it. Aunt Lou, put the potatoes in a pot of cold water. Except the one I got blood on.

(To herself, raising her bloodied fist, and taking deep breaths.) Hold it above the heart. Come on, ice cube. Make it numb. Ice. Iceberg. Glacier. A big Alaskan glacier ... on my finger. Kissing my finger, making the pain go away. Glaciers. Snow, soft white drifts, like waves of icing on a wedding cake, like ...

... Leonard Bemstein's hair. The summer I was eleven, and Reuben took me to Tanglewood. They remembered him, all the older musicians did, from when he played there. First clarinet. Reuben told them he was just teaching now and I was his star pupil. But they knew. It was a hot day, and when a drinker sweats, you can just smell it on them. We all could.

And then, this ... this wave of energy comes at us, and it's Leonard Bernstein. "Reuben! Reuben, God, where the hell have you been? Reuben, dear, darling, Reuben." And Leonard Bernstein's hugging Reuben and kissing him. Kissing! Then, Reuben says, "Lenny"—to Leonard Bernstein!—he says, "Lenny, this is Ainsley Belcher, my star pupil. She plays the clarinet." And then ...

(She lowers the wounded hand, as if it's being held by Leonard Bernstein.)

Leonard Bernstein kisses my hand! Can't look him in the eye, or I'll sink like the Titanic. So I'm looking at his hair, these waves of thick, soft, white hair. Like snow. Big, soft, Alaskan glaciers.

They call rehearsal, and "Lenny" looks up at me, and quotes Lord Byron, my favorite poet!

"Maid of Athens, ere we part,
Give, oh give me back my heart."

And he left. For three hours I sat on the grass watching rehearsal, and didn't move a muscle or even go to the bathroom, even when the orchestra took a break. I didn't move.

(She hums a passage from Beethoven's Ode to Joy, *"conducting" with the wounded hand.)*

After that, when I practiced up in the cake room, if my cheeks hurt, or the muscles in my jaw got tired, I couldn't feel it. Leonard Bernstein was there. Conducting. Kissing my...

(Her hand.) It doesn't hurt anymore.

Moby Ethan at the Sculptor's Museum

Constance Congdon

(Scene begins in the dark. Suddenly, a flashlight is turned on, revealing the chin and face of ETHAN. He's holding the flashlight under his chin so that the effect is eerie.)

ETHAN *(in a performance-like tone)*. Call me Ishmael.

(In his normal voice, looking for the trustee with his flashlight.)

So, do you like that, Mrs. Chapin-Skinner? Because I could do something as good for the life of Mr. Daniel French if I thought about how I could illustrate the work of a sculptor. I could be holding a chisel or I could, like, cover myself with white flour and stand, like I was—check this out—like I was—could you turn on the light, Mrs. Chapin-Skinner?

(Lights up on ETHAN. He is standing in his jockey shorts.)

I think we need to, like, decide, whether or not I'm going to be the sculptor or the sculpture. *Or*, I could just sit in a chair, in a suit, with a beard on—get where I'm going with this? And impersonate that sculpture of Abraham Lincoln over there. That might take less prep time. You see, at the Melville house I just recite a lot of *Moby-Dick*, or, if I hate the people I'm guiding, I recite *Pierre or The Ambiguities* and that usually gets them out of the house, so I can lock up and bike back to Stockbridge to catch the before-dinner tour of the Rockwell Museum. Because I need the money, of course.

(Lights go out. Sound of a scuffle.)

Mrs. Chapin-Skinner! What are you doing? Good God!

(Breaking away.) Now this is just not right, so let go of me—let GO!

(Sound of a crash. ETHAN turns on his flashlight and investigates.)

Jesus! What have you done?? Mrs. Chapin-Skinner?? Look at this!! You have knocked over the Daniel French Museum Official Replica of the Abraham Lincoln Memorial Statue!! Ohmygod!! It's chipped!! Oh man! I am so fired!! Prudence!! Prudence!! You have been a very bad trustee tonight. If one cannot trust a trustee, then—YOU HAVE BELIED THE NAME OF TRUSTEE!!! YOU DO NOT DESERVE TO BE A TRUSTEE OF THE DANIEL FRENCH MUSEUM OR ANY MUSEUM!! MRS. CHAPIN-SKINNER, GET YOUR HANDS OFF OF MY PANTS!!! *JESUS!!*

(He flails at his assailant with his flashlight, until he drops it and he's in complete darkness again.)

Mrs. Chapin-Skinner? Are you all right? Prudence? Pru? I didn't mean to hit you that hard. Squeeze my hand if you can hear my voice. Just squeeze—

(But she squeezes his genitals.)

Ohmygod. Ohmygod. Ohmygod. Mrs. Chapin-Skinner, what are you doing now? Did you take out your teeth? Ahhh. Ahhhh. Ahhhhh. Call me Ishmael! Call me—ohhh, ohhh, ohhhhhhhh! Just call me, call me, call me! YESSSSSSSSS!

(He climaxes. Beat.)

Ooooo. Uh.

(Beat.)

Did you ever play the oboe, Mrs. Chapin-Skinner? Because you certainly have the lips for it. My sister says it takes really strong lips.

Turn Down

Shirley Lauro

(AINSLEY at desk reading letter she's writing. Crumpled paper on floor.)

AINSLEY *(warm, familial tone).* Dr. Rudolph Silensky, Chairman, Admissions Committee, Boston Conservatory of Music.... Dear Dr. Silensky, *First,* let me express my happiness and great appreciation to the entire audition committee for selecting me at the Conservatory in the Woodwind Division for next fall. My deepest dream has come true...

(She stops at the end of the part she's written, thinks, then starts to write.)

Second, I—

(Stops, goes on.) Is there any possibility of a late admission? Postponing until... *(Crosses this out, starts again.)*

However, since my audition, I— *(Crosses this out.)*

Unfortunately, however, now—until—

(Stops abruptly, tears sheet from pad, crumples it, throws to floor. Gathers strength, starts over, much more formal, distant tone.)

Dear Dr. Silensky ... I want to inform the Committee that although ... I am honored ... to have been chosen for admission—

(She stops again, then determined pushes on:)

A deep family responsibility and commitment ... make it ... impossible for me to accept ... at this time ...

(Close to tears, she stops, stifles them, goes on:)

Thank you all for your consideration and—faith—in my talent—and ... *me* ...

(She breaks, sobbing, finishing:)

Sincerely ... Ainsley Belcher—

(She puts letter in envelope. A beat. She goes to the phone, dials number she's written down on desk.)

Danville Correctional Facility? Yes—we spoke before? Ainsley Belcher? My brother Ethan. Right—hitchhiking and alcohol level—right. Well, *I'm* coming, so please tell the officers in charge there? I want a meeting. Right off the turnpike you said, didn't you? So a couple of hours. *My* custody ... the responsible adult ... yes ... well, with our mother ... but she works every night ... *I'm* home.

Yes, and I'll straighten it out... he's an exceptional boy and this is just a fluke of some kind... so if you'll tell who's in charge about a meeting... thank you...

(Hangs up, starts out, remembers letter, gets it, looking at it a moment.)

Misadventure

Donald Margulies

(The parking lot of the Danville, New Hampshire, police station. AINSLEY's fuming. ETHAN's sheepish. It's cold.)

AINSLEY *(to policeman offstage; laced with sarcasm).* Thank you, Officer. Thanks a lot. *(To ETHAN.)* Get in the car.

ETHAN *(refusing).* Un-uh.

AINSLEY. Get. In. The. Car.

ETHAN. No way.

AINSLEY. Ethan! Get in the car!

ETHAN. I refuse to get in the car when you're like this.

AINSLEY. Like what?

ETHAN. You're mad at me.

AINSLEY. I am not mad at you.

ETHAN. Yes you are; I can tell: Your nostrils are doing that thing.

AINSLEY. What thing?

ETHAN. *You* know, they kinda... *(He demonstrates by flaring his nostrils.)*

AINSLEY. GETINTHECAR!

ETHAN. What if you lose control and crash into a tree or something?

AINSLEY. I'm not gonna lose control.

ETHAN. How do *you* know? You might get this uncontrollable urge to smack me repeatedly, and *then* what?

AINSLEY. I am not gonna smack you! Get in the car!

ETHAN. I've had enough trauma for one evening, thank you.

AINSLEY. *You've* had enough trauma?!

ETHAN. Yes! The stigma of incarceration will haunt me for years.

AINSLEY *(softly)*. Get in the car. *(He shakes his head.)* Ethan, I am too tired and too pissed off—

ETHAN. Ah ha! *(She let her anger slip.)*

AINSLEY *(continuous)*. —to be having this argument with you in a police station parking lot in Nowhere, New Hampshire. I'm cold and I want to go home.

ETHAN. I like the cold; the cold feels good. It's sobering me up. I feel more awake than I've ever felt in my life.

AINSLEY. What were you *thinking*?! What in the world were you *thinking*?!

ETHAN. I don't know.

AINSLEY. You don't *know*? Were you trying to *kill* yourself? Huh? Were you?

(He shrugs.)

ETHAN. No. I don't know. Maybe.

AINSLEY. Maybe?! MAYBE?!

ETHAN. I don't *know*, I said.

AINSLEY. You selfish boy! You stupid selfish boy!

ETHAN. Good. Let it out. I'm glad we're talking now; it's much better then that nostril thing.

AINSLEY. How DARE you be reckless with your life! How DARE you!

ETHAN. Shhh! You're disturbing the peace. You want them to throw *both* of us in jail?

AINSLEY. What's *my* life worth if you trash yours? Huh? Have you thought about that?!! I'll have to live the next seventy-five years haunted every goddamn day by your pimply, ghostly self! We're not just sibs, you stupid moron, we're soul mates! Don't you know that by now?!

ETHAN *(childlike, surprised by the depth of her rage, he nods; a beat, softly)*. I'm sorry.

AINSLEY. You drink yourself sick and go hitching on the Interstate?! Are you crazy?! Have I taught you nothing?!

ETHAN. Hey. A. I said I was sorry.

AINSLEY. Never mind being drunk and weaving on the shoulder with cars and trucks whizzing by at eighty miles an hour! Never mind that! What if a crazy person stopped to pick you up—a Jeffrey Dahmer-type or something—

ETHAN *(amused)*. What?!

AINSLEY. —and took you away so you were never heard from again! Some Boy Scouts would come across your jaw bone one day in the woods! It's a good thing the cops picked you up and threw you in jail. You could've been roadkill!

ETHAN. You're nuts, you know that? You've been watching too much television.

AINSLEY. Don't mock me! There ARE crazy people out there, you know, they're not just CREATED by the media, they exist! There are truly bad and sick people out there in the world who want nothing more than to destroy other people's happiness! *(He cracks up.)* Stop laughing! STOP IT!! It isn't funny! You scared me, Ethan! You scared me to death!!

(She throws punches at him; he protects his head with his hands, laughing until she really hurts him.)

ETHAN. Ow!

(She stops. Silence.)

That hurt.

AINSLEY. Good.

ETHAN. I can explain.

AINSLEY. Nothing you could possibly say...

ETHAN. Aren't you even gonna give me my due process? Aren't you?

AINSLEY. I don't see why I should.

ETHAN. I'm just a kid, you know.

AINSLEY. Oh, God. Is that your excuse? Is that your piss-ant excuse?!

ETHAN. Kids are *supposed* to act out and do reckless things. Right? If not while I'm young, when? When I'm old? When I'm forty?

AINSLEY. The key is surviving long enough to attain wisdom.

ETHAN. Okay, so let's chalk it up to the folly of youth. Okay? I've learned my lesson: I drank a whole lot of really shitty bourbon with some asshole I don't even like whose approval I inexplicably crave and blew Pizza Hut pizza all down my front and onto my brand new running shoes. Don't you think I'm humiliated enough? I just *bought* these shoes. Like a week ago.

AINSLEY. If you'd *killed* yourself...! If you'd gotten yourself killed for some stupid, peer-pressure, macho, adolescent, alcoholic misadventure.... If I'd *lost* you 'cause of it.... If I'd *lost* you...

(She finally lets herself weep; she turns away from him. He's impressed. Silence.)

Pizza Hut, huh. No wonder you smell like a dairy farmer.

ETHAN. I can't even smell it anymore.

AINSLEY. Trust me.

ETHAN. Oh, yeah, why should I trust *you*?

AINSLEY. Because you'd better. Because if you don't trust *me*, brother, you are a goner. You are toast. *(A beat.)* Now get in the car.

ETHAN. Still mad at me?

AINSLEY *(smiling)*. Get in the fucking car?

ETHAN *(smiles; a beat, as he gets into the car)*. Can we stop somewhere to get something to eat? I'm starving.

AINSLEY. We'll see. Phew. You stink.

(She starts the car.)

Something To Do With Bolivia

Jon Klein

(ETHAN sits on the front steps of the post office at Harper's Ferry, writing a very large postcard. The discarded remains of previous attempts lie in a torn pile at his feet.

He has a noticeably black eye.

He pauses, squinting down at his writing, rereading something.)

ETHAN. Shit. Careful, bro. This is from Mr. Spring Fling.

(He tears it in half and throws it on the pile. He starts over with a new card.)

Dear Ainsley ...

(Lights up on AINSLEY, reading the postcard.)

How's it goin'? Bet you thought I forgot you, but how could I ever forget you? You think I'd spend four weeks off trail with any girl who'd give me a lift to the grocery? Guess who I ran into down at Harper's Ferry. Your brother Ethan. Small world, huh. He was on some cheap rail pass, takin' on some history, and I just came off the Appalachian Trail. So we're shootin' the shit, and he tells me you been wonderin' what the hell happened to me. Man, was I glad to see your brother.

(ETHAN gingerly rubs his black eye.) Dickwad.

(He resumes.) The thing is, I quit the postcards 'cause I... lost my pen.

(He stops, looking at his pen.) Damn.

(He gets an idea.) Till now. Ta-da! The thing is, Ethan said it reminded you of your dad's postcards, how they stopped without any warning. And you said what is it about men that they all need "time to think." But the truth is, guys *don't* need time to think. It's just that they can only think about one thing at a time. Take the old dude on this postcard—John Brown. Talk about a one-track mind. He fought off the entire U.S. Army from a little stone firehouse—just like the end of *Butch Cassidy*. Because all he could think about was slavery, just like all Butch could think about was Bolivia, and all Captain Ahab could think about was a big stupid whale. Add it all up, and what do you get? No justice, foreign territory, and a really long fishing trip. Hi, Dad.

(AINSLEY frowns. ETHAN thinks about that, and scratches out the last two words. He resumes.)

Anyways, right now all I can think about is this trail, and getting to Georgia. I guess that's a little like Bolivia too. But I... miss you, babe. You were the first. I promise.

(AINSLEY beams, enraptured. ETHAN stops writing.) Fat chance, you prick.

(He resumes.) One last thing. Give your brother a break. I know you think he's a dumb shit, but he hates to see you get hurt, which is why he came here to punch my fucking lights out...

(AINSLEY stands up, furious.)

Shit.

(Lights out on AINSLEY. ETHAN tears the card in two and throws it on the pile. He pulls out another large postcard.)

Dear Ainsley...

Or Maybe Not

Adele Edling Shank

(AINSLEY, sitting on the front porch after supper, talking to the frogs.)

AINSLEY. I knew Mr. Harnette would be mad, but I didn't think he'd be, like, fireworks. Pouff. Pouff. Anger lighting up the sky. I knew he'd be awful sorry I'm not going, but there was no call for him to... he didn't have to say words like coward. Nobody ever called me a coward. I got the strength to go, all right. I'm tough enough, all right. He oughta ask that cop who put Ethan in jail if I'm tough. "I'm just trying to teach 'im a lesson." Well I let him know what I thought of lessons like that at about a hundred and thirty decibels and he goes, "Stop, stop! You gotta voice like an ax, my head is splittin'." So there Mr.-Harnette-think-you-know-so-much-about-me, you ask that cop if I got a spine or not. And you ask that basketball coaching English teacher who wrote "moron" on Ethan's essay about my spine. He got a hundred and sixty decibels and the diabolicalest headache ever was! Yeah, Mr.-Harnette-think-you-got-me-pegged, you ask him if I'm a coward. And the dumb shit kid Jimmy, I almost made his brain explode when I found out he sold Ethan acid. Ask Jimmy if I've got a spine or not! And if I can take on a cop and a basketball coach and a drug dealer, I can stand up to a few musicians in Boston for sure!!

So, it's pretty clear to me we aren't at all talking about my spine here. It's not a question of how tough I am. It's a question... It's more a question of... Okay, I don't really know what it's a question of. I guess...I guess... Maybe I'm only tough enough for Ethan. Maybe I'm not tough enough for me.

Things don't feel right anymore. I can't remember when they stopped feeling right, it's been so long. Suppose I didn't notice at the time. Or maybe I thought it was just a temporary dip. Now it feels like the Grand Canyon. And I can't figure out how to get things feeling right again. Maybe now I finally made the big decision, now I know I'm staying home with Ethan, maybe now I'll get some peace, and maybe things will feel right again. Or maybe not.

Dead Men Make No Dollars

Val Smith

(Lights up on ETHAN, sitting in a puddle of water, dressed in wet suit, mask and flippers sans tanks. He partially unzips the front of the suit. A cascade of golf balls pours out. He blows a golf ball out of his mouth.)

ETHAN. Yes, Willis, I went down into the duck pond. I took that risk. At midnight, yes. It was dark so the golfers finally went home, okay? And I had a few beers because a relaxed focus was called for. Calculated risk. Okay? *(Pause.)* Dangerous, well. We both know I ran out of oxygen. I got excited. Understandably so. *(Pause.)* I AM grateful you pulled my ass out. I'm not arguing that. What I am arguing is that underlying MY action, which you so cavalierly refer to as "yet another of my scary dumbass escapades" is the all-American capitalistic belief in independence. Financial gain READ independence. I do not wish to die. I, Willis, wish to make a *killing*. If anyone has a death wish around here, Willis, it's you. An *insincere* death wish to be sure, but a death wish however incompetently expressed is still a death wish.

(Long pause. Listens to Willis.) Okay. Fine. *Let's* talk about it. Specifico numero uno. You open your mother's medicine cabinet. There is a bottle marked "Valium."

There is another bottle marked "Aspirin." Which one do YOU, who can read, and who SINCERELY wishes to kill himself, choose?

Ejemplo number dos. Room full of people concentrating intensely on that fine, fine actress, Cameron Diaz in that superb film, *Something About Mary*. You walk through the room carrying a rope. It becomes obvious you are going to hang yourself. It becomes obvious you are going to use the so-called "chandelier" in your mother's dining room. Now, Willis, it wasn't that we cared more about Cameron Diaz than you. But anybody with half a fuckin' brain knows that wrought iron dangle hanging from the cottage cheese in your mother's dining room probably cost the builder all of two dollars and fifty cents. With luck, it might support a balloon.

Ejemplo three. If you are going to use a rifle to shoot yourself, Willis, what do you do? Do you put it in your ear? Do you put it in your mouth? No. YOU decide that the most effective way to kill yourself is to take aim and I quote, "sever the artery that runs down the neck from the brain over to the shoulder." Unquote. Fuck me. So now, your mother has a plywood board over her bay window, a giant hole in her dining room ceiling and you have a chipped collar bone. And, Willis, Willis—follow me here, *you are still alive.*

Yes, I too am still alive. Yes, thanks to you. Okay, okay. Bastando, awright?

Truce. Okay. So. I will give up my shit IF you give up your shit. I will give up the most unbelievable underwater gold mine since, since, fucking... King Tut's tomb.

(Points to golf ball.) Look, Willis. A Titleist. Near virgin condition.

(Throwing golf balls back in the pond. And another. And finally, he throws one at Willis and laughs.)

Shit, Willis.

The Deal

Jane Martin

(AINSLEY sits at a kitchen table with nine glass-bottled beers on it.)

AINSLEY. I never drank nine beers before. I feel strangely free. Ethan, bring me my toe out of the refrigerator, will you? I like to see my toe when I'm drunk.

(ETHAN brings the toe. It's in a Ziplock sandwich bag.)

Thanks. Two and a half years old, an' I cut this baby clean off with a snow shovel the night Mama went to the hospital to have you. You ingrate. One of a thousand sacrifices, baby brother. If ol' Reuben hadn't a come along drunk as a lord, I might have bled to death, but, more importantly, I would never, never have played the oboe. Did you know Reuben played with the Boston Symphony Orchestra for thirty years? That old drunk, who would have thought it. He's got crystal pure tone. You play a duet with Reuben, you downright feel fucked. He's eighty-one years old come November.

(She opens the Ziplock and dumps the toe into her hand.)

They sewed this baby on an' it lasted fourteen years till it snapped off that time I fell when I was doing cross-country. I believe the moral to be that you can't put something broken back together. Not in the long run. This has proved true in all three of my romantic relationships. In each one, we split an' then came back together an' then broke off forever. The toe knows.

(She puts it back in the bag.)

I wonder how it came to be that I'm a supporting role even in my own life. I mean I thought I'd star in my life, but it hasn't worked out that way. You're the star of my life, brother mine. Whatever I am it's in relation to you. Second oboe. You know people hear about my toe before they hear about me? I meet 'em an' they say, "Oh, sure, you're the one keeps her toe in the refrigerator." Second fiddle to my own body parts. At what point, Ethan, is it determined in your life whether you are to be a first chair or just a general all-purpose oboist? I believe it was when you were born, Ethan, and I wasn't allowed to go to the hospital. I was not ... among the chosen, though I did, however, achieve self-mutilation with the snow shovel. Well, "They also serve who only bleed and wait," right? I believe I'll put my claim to fame back in the freezer compartment and fix you some dinner. What, dearest Ethan, would you like for dinner? I was once offered admission to the Boston Conservatory of Music, and though our family mythology would have it that I gave it up on your behalf, my sad, wild brother, I actually declined on the basis that it was a hell of a lot of money just to come out playing second oboe. It seemed a ... pretension to be expensively trained to be ordinary. Oh, it's best to know who you are ... or so they tell you.

Blackfish

Courtney Baron

(ETHAN stands with a bucket of ice—fish inside.)

ETHAN. Women want to know how you got to be the way you are. Like screening for mental illness. A litmus test to make sure you're not going to get worse. You want to check out the closet before you put your nice clothes inside. I think I love my girlfriend. I know my illness, my crime, but I tell her, "My father left us for fish," took an extended ichthyological adventure. And that does fuck with me. But it's not my crime. This is a fish.

(He holds up the bucket.)

Seven years ago it's Christmas and Ainsley is wearing these tiny ornament earrings. I'm driving us home. She sings Christmas songs and I say, "Your mouth is a cathedral." This is an Alaskan Blackfish.

(He pulls a blackfish from the bucket.)

Ainsley wants to go home, but I have this magnet and it draws me to Lake Onota. She shows me the North Star and I tell her I know where Jesus is. You're wondering why I want to go to the lake in the middle of the fucking night. I'm drawn to where the fish are. But it's not my crime.

(He puts down the bucket and looks at the fish.)

Ainsley says I wouldn't know Jesus if he bit me in the ass. I don't know why, but this pisses me off and I shove her back in the truck. Now she's pissed too. She's holding on to the dash as we pass the cardboard nativity at the neighbors, I say, "See there's Jesus." And she cracks this smile, her smile, because kneeling in front of the plastic-baby-away-in-a-manger Jesus is Santa Claus. I'm laughing so hard, I barely feel the thud as I pull into our drive. I jump out to see what I've run over. The neighbor's old Doberman is lying at Ainsley's feet. I've run over it. Ainsley's sparkling, those ornament earrings. I say, "You look like a Christmas tree." She says there's a gift at her feet. Ainsley bends down and says that the dog is breathing. I think, "Your mouth is a cathedral. Bless me." And she's got tears and the dog whimpers and I don't know why but her disappointment kills me. I die. She watches me freeze. And I wait for her to forgive me. She pulls me down to the dog and she puts my hand in hers and runs it through the dog's fur. And I'm born again.

(He runs his hand over the fish.)

The Alaskan blackfish freezes in the water every winter, freezes dead. And every summer it thaws out and lives again. Ainsley's disappointment freezes me. Then she grabs my hand and I'm revived. You can't tell this to your girlfriend. You can't say that you love your sister more than life, that Ainsley makes me an Alaskan blackfish. I die and live over and over again for her. My father left us for fishing in Alaska. But the fish is here. I can't tell you why I know that if he had stayed I wouldn't breathe for Ainsley. But I do. I breathe for Ainsley. I'm a fish dying and reviving over again. It's the perfect crime. I'm a fish.

Star Skating

John Olive

(AINSLEY enters, pulling on a robe. She opens the door and ETHAN enters, shivering from the cold, stomping the floor, eyes burning from sleeplessness.)

ETHAN. I went skating on the reservoir last night. It was amazing. The whole reservoir was smooth as ebony. Black. A mirror. It was like skating on stars. *(Laughs.)* I felt like a fish swimming upside down following Ethan Belcher as he soared and swooped under the stars. If I could just break through the ice I could fly. Did Kimmy call?

(AINSLEY shakes her head.)

She didn't? That's... Well, that's okay. She's sleeping probably. We had an interesting night. *(Takes off his jacket, sits near AINSLEY.)* Here's what it is. We keep our lives small. You know, in these tight patterns with very familiar players: you, Mom, Aunt Lou, Reuben, and Kimmy, and I used to think it was because I was afraid, of... not change so much as of breaking through the ice and discovering that, yes, the stars are much brighter out in the cold air which, oh shit, I now discover I can't breathe. Know what I mean? *(Laughs again.)*

But that's not it. We keep our lives small so we can hear magic scratching at the door. If we're living too big, or we're distracted by the sound of money and our tantrumming little egos, we might miss it. All this time I was waiting for it and now I heard it so of course I had to go skating. *(Looks at AINSLEY.)* Did I wake you up?

(Suddenly stands.) I should take a shower. Is it too early to call Kimmy? Yeah, she should sleep. It's just that, well, you think I'm not clear now, you shoulda heard me last night. *(Laughs.)*

I slept, maybe, half an hour. I had such wild dreams, like nightmares but I always woke up laughing. Except one. I dreamed I was back on the reservoir skating and as I looked down into the black sky there was a huge bird above me, matching me move for move, swoop for swoop, but when I stopped and looked up... The sky was empty. That dream made me cry.

(A beat.) It's too early to call Kimmy. I can't wake her up. I'm too shivery to shower. Tummy's too tense for coffee. It's gonna snow today.

(Looks at AINSLEY.) What're we gonna do?

(A moment. Then AINSLEY stands, goes to ETHAN, takes his head in her hands and kisses him.)

AINSLEY. We'll clean out the cake room and put in a crib.

Barbra Live at Canyon Ranch

Tanya Palmer

(AINSLEY enters with a clipboard and a towel over her shoulder. A woman, Barbra Streisand, is lying on her stomach on a massage table. AINSLEY moves toward the table and begins to speak.)

AINSLEY. Ms. Streisand? I've got you down here for a Lymphatic Balancing Massage, but Jeannie's locked up all the aromatherapy bottles in the cabinet and I can't find a key. So it looks like the Stress Buster for you!

(Putting down the clipboard.) Just let me know if I'm doing it too hard. And no speaking, please, we find it creates tension in the sternocleidomastoid muscles. *(Pause.)*

I have to tell you, we were all pretty excited when we heard you were coming to Canyon Ranch; Richie at the front desk is a HUGE fan. He performed "Woman in Love" at the talent show last summer and won first prize. He looks just like you, when he dresses up, down to the nails and everything. Okay, now this is the part where I really go for it, so don't be scared.

(She starts whaling on Barbra's back, takes a deep breath, then goes back to moving slowly.)

Isn't that just the best feeling, Babs? Do you mind if I call you Babs? That's what my great-aunt Lou calls you so that's how I think of you. Aunt Lou was thrilled when I told her you were a guest here. She said that girl is a real talent and a class act! I told her that you were very polite except for the fact that you were always changing your massage appointment, which caused a few problems with scheduling and staff. But Lou said, listen Ainsley, that woman sings, she dances, she acts, she directs, she produces and she looks great doing it and I think that entitles her to change her massage appointment a few times. She argued so passionately that she almost convinced me. Okay, Babs, now I'm moving down to the lower back, where I'm going to stimulate and balance the body's immune system through gentle strokes with the fingertips. *(Pause.)*

I'm musical myself, although I don't sing. Did you always know that you wanted to entertain? I think you have to really want to if you're going to make it to the top. For me, music is more private, a way of saying things that are really personal, things that are hard to put into words. Sometimes I have conversations with music. Conversations with people who aren't there. I know that sounds weird, but I think you understand. Like that scene in *Yentl* when you're out in the woods just after you've hacked off your hair. You're on your way to the Yeshiva and you're looking up at the stars and singing to your dead father. *(Sings.)* "Papa, can you hear me?" *(Pause.)*

It's weird, isn't it, that we keep trying to bring them back, like they're this magic ingredient that will make our life whole. I mean, at least in *Yentl* your dad was really nice and supportive. My dad didn't do much. He was okay, but he sure didn't instruct me in the Talmud or anything like that! Still, I wish I'd wake up and find he was home. *(Sings.)* "Papa, can you hear me? Papa, can you see me?" What'd ya think Barbra? Babs? Do you think he can?

Introducing Dad

Susan Miller

(ETHAN stands next to his unborn baby's newly assembled crib. He is nervous, in awe, and trying to find words of introduction to a life on the way.)

ETHAN. Okay. Okay. Okay. I've been trying to think of something to tell you, our first time alone like this. Well, my first time alone with the idea of you. I mean—about how to be.

(Beat.)

Hey, this used to be the cake room. You're in with the cakes now. There were hundreds of them nobody ever showed up for. We moved them out to make room for you. I used to hide in here when I was a kid, wondering why they weren't picked up. Who'd've left them like that? You could get crazy thinking about it. The wedding cakes, especially. Suddenly a girl wakes up and knows it's over. Leaves him, leaves the white frosting, a nice life. There was this chocolate layer for some Jimmy guy's high school graduation. Jimmy, we believe in you, it said. Jimmy, you did it, it said. Did they just stop believing in him? Is that why they left his cake here? Why would anyone want to leave something so sweet and perfect behind. Except, I guess, if it reminded you of something you failed at or didn't live up to.

(Beat.)

You don't even have a name yet. I mean, what do we call a thing like you? It's just ... there's no word. There's no word for you. I want to give you a name nobody else has. *Cake*. Or—or—*Batter*. Maybe, *Icing*. *Flash*. What do you think? You're not talking but you're not quiet, either. You are a noise. You're the biggest sound in the universe.

(Beat.)

I want to tell you things. I used to be full of what to say. But I can't make you up. I have to get you right.

(Beat.)

You don't know me, but I know you. You are crazy beautiful. You are brilliant. You're gonna be right here sleeping in this room. With actual skin. And hands. This is a person coming. This is everything.

(Suddenly inspired.)

I want to name you *Story*.

(Beat.)

I don't know what a father's supposed to do, exactly. But I'm going to stay and find out.

(Beat.)

Tell me how to do it right.

Norman Rockwell's Thanksgiving in the Year 2000

Joan Ackermann

(They sit at a kitchen table. AINSLEY is relaxed, content, working on a letter.)

ETHAN *(earnestly)*. Read it again.

AINSLEY. Did you just fart?

ETHAN. No.

AINSLEY. You did.

ETHAN. I didn't.

AINSLEY: You did.

ETHAN. Well. It's Thanksgiving.

AINSLEY. Oh right.

ETHAN. Read it again.

AINSLEY. "Dear Jim ... "

ETHAN. Maybe we should say ... "Dear Dad."

AINSLEY. We never do.

ETHAN. We don't?

AINSLEY. No.

ETHAN. Oh.

AINSLEY. "Dear Jim ... "

ETHAN. We never write to him. *(She looks at him.)* So we never write "Dear Jim" or "Dear Dad."

AINSLEY. We've written to him.

ETHAN. When?

AINSLEY. Ethan...

ETHAN. I think we should say "Dear Dad." In honor of the occasion.

AINSLEY. Thanksgiving?

ETHAN. No. Me becoming. A dad. *(AINSLEY stares at him.)* What. *What.*

AINSLEY. I'm just... assimilating. Your news. "Dear Dad... Happy Thanksgiving."

ETHAN. Do we have his address?

AINSLEY. We have his address from... a few years ago. It should still work.

ETHAN. What if it doesn't?

AINSLEY. His loss. "We've had a terrific Thanksgiving."

ETHAN. What do you think they eat for Thanksgiving in Alaska?

AINSLEY. Turkey. "Lou came downstairs for the occasion. She pretty much stays in bed most of the time now. Reuben, you will remember, our tenant..." *(Pondering the phrasing.)* You will remember. You *will* remember "made stuffing with roasted artichoke hearts." And now Ethan is farting them out his ears. Just kidding, "You won't believe it but we finally cleared out the cake room. We need the space. Ethan's girlfriend Kimmy is going to have a baby and she's moving in. She's going to work for Mom in her video store." We should cross that out, right? A reference to Mom? *(Shrugs.)* Eh. Leave it in. "Thought you'd like to know. You're going to be a grandfather. Congratulations. Ethan and Ainsley." *(She looks at him. His eyes are tearing up.)* What's wrong? Ethan. What's wrong, sweetie?

ETHAN. I don't know. Nothing.

AINSLEY. Nothing? Your face is red, your eyes are watery.

ETHAN. I don't know. I'm happy ... I'm ... *(He shakes his head, throws up his arms. Grins, doesn't know what he is.)* It was ... nice of you.

AINSLEY. What.

ETHAN. To say Kimmy should move in. That was ... I appreciate it.

AINSLEY. Stop. Your gas is going to your head. So, were you guys using birth control at all?

ETHAN. At all?

AINSLEY *(just stares at him, knowing the answer)*. What do you think they eat for Thanksgiving in Alaska?

ETHAN. Uh ... I don't know if there are turkeys there. If they migrated over that ... strait.

AINSLEY. That strait? The Bering Strait? You mean from Russia?

ETHAN. No. *(Pause.)*

AINSLEY. So. Are we sending this? This okay?

ETHAN. Should we say some more?

AINSLEY. What more?

ETHAN. I don't know.

AINSLEY. You're a mess tonight.

ETHAN. Yeah.

AINSLEY. Let's eat some pie.

ETHAN. I finished it.

AINSLEY. You finished the pie?

ETHAN. Ainsley. You're my saving grace.

AINSLEY. Is that like *Saving Private Ryan*? You finished the pie?

ETHAN. Without you ... I don't think I'd be alive.

AINSLEY. There was half a pie left.

ETHAN. I'm sorry.

AINSLEY *(looks over her shoulder)*. What's that noise?

ETHAN. There's a gutter loose. I'll fix it tomorrow. *(Pause.)*

AINSLEY. I'm gonna start a vegetable garden this spring, back where there's all that dead brush. I'm gonna clear it out and plant a whole bunch of vegetables.

ETHAN. You want me to go to Price Chopper and buy you a pie?

AINSLEY. No.

ETHAN. I will.

AINSLEY. Price Chopper is closed.

ETHAN. We could make one.

AINSLEY. I don't know why I'm hungry.

ETHAN. Do we have the ingredients?

AINSLEY. For another pumpkin pie? Actually, we do.

ETHAN. Let's make one.

AINSLEY. Okay.

ETHAN. Let's tell Jim... We're making a pie. Write that. Post script. P.S.

AINSLEY. P.S. We're making a pie?

ETHAN. Yeah.

AINSLEY. All right. *(She writes.)* P.S. We're making a pie. At midnight. In your mother's oven. Come on over.

ETHAN. That's nice. That's good.

(He wipes a tear from his eye. AINSLEY reaches over and grabs his hand.)

AINSLEY. Ethan, you are *my* saving grace.

END OF PLAY

About the Playwrights

Joan Ackermann is Co-Artistic Director of Mixed Company in Great Barrington, Massachusetts, a year-round theatre now in its 18th year. Her plays include *Zara Spook and Other Lures* (1990 Humana Festival of New American Plays), *Stanton's Garage* (1993 Humana Festival), *The Batting Cage* (1996 Humana Festival), *Don't Ride the Clutch, Yonder Peasant, Bed and Breakfast, The Light of His Eye, Rescuing Greenland, Off the Map, My New York Hit, Marcus Is Walking* and her most recent play, *Isabella*, a musical for which she composed the music. Before writing plays, Ackermann was a journalist for 10 years and wrote for *Sports Illustrated, Time, The Atlantic, Esquire, GQ, Audubon, New York* and other magazines.

Courtney Baron's 10-minute play *The Blue Room* premiered at the 1999 Humana Festival. Other productions include *Dear Anton* (Chekhov Now Festival), *You Are Not Forgotten* (workshop at the Royal Court Theatre, London), *Dream of Heaven and Hell* (Walkerspace, New York), *The Good Night* (Theatre for the New City, New York), *Love as a Science* (Seattle Fringe Festival), *Clip* (Frontera Fest) and *The White Girl and the Sheep* (Theatre Three, Dallas). In 1998, Baron received her M.F.A. from the Columbia University Playwriting Program.

Neena Beber was most recently at Actors Theatre of Louisville with her ten-minute play *Misreadings* (included in Best American Short Plays, 1996-97). *A Common Vision* and *The Brief but Exemplary Life of the Living Goddess* both premiered at the Magic Theatre; *Tomorrowland* at New Georges and subsequently Theatre J in Washington, D.C.; *Failure to Thrive* at Padua Hills Playwrights Festival. One acts *Adaptive Ruse, Departures* and *Sensation(s)* at HB Playwrights Foundation; *Acts of Desire*, collected shorts, Watermark Theatre. Her new plays *Thirst* and *Hard Feelings* were developed at Ojai Playwrights

Conference, Williamstown Theatre Festival, Otterbein and the Public Theater's New Work Now. Additional credits include an Amblin Commission from Playwrights Horizons, A.S.K. Exchange to The Royal Court, and a Distinguished Alumni Award from New York University's Tisch School of the Arts. *Bad Dates*, a film, is based on her one-act play, *Food*. Beber holds a B.A. from Harvard. She is a member of New Dramatists.

Constance Congdon's works include *Tales of the Lost Formicans*, which premiered at the Humana Festival and has had more than 100 productions, *Lips*, *So Far*, *Losing Father's Body*, *Dark Bridge Mountain*, *The Automata Pietà*, *Casanova*, which premiered at the New York Shakespeare Festival, and *Dog Opera*, which was commissioned by the New York Shakespeare Festival. Congdon also wrote the libretto for a new opera by Peter Gordon, *The Strange Life of Ivan Osokin*, as well as the libretti for two operas by Ron Perera, *S* and *The Yellow Wallpaper*. She has written seven plays for the Children's Theatre of Minneapolis. A collection of Congdon's plays is published by the Theatre Communications Group, Inc. Other plays include *Native American*, *No Mercy*, *The Gilded Age*, and *One Day Earlier* (a companion piece for *No Mercy*). Congdon's plays have been produced in Moscow, Helsinki, Hong Kong, Edinburgh and London, as well as in over 50 regional and university theaters in the United States.

Jon Klein is the author of 20 produced plays, which have been produced off-Broadway and at such major regional theaters as South Coast Repertory, Arena Stage, Alley Theatre, Alliance Theatre, Center Stage and A Contemporary Theatre. Actors Theatre of Louisville productions include *Betty the Yeti* and *T Bone N Weasel* (HBO New Plays USA Award; film version on TNT). Other plays: *Dimly Perceived Threats to the System*, *Octopus*, *Peoria*, *Four Our Fathers*, *Southern Cross* and *Losing It* (Dramatists Guild/CBS New Play Award). Stage adaptations: Stendhal's *The Red and the Black*, two *Hardy Boys* adventures and *Bunnicula*. Upcoming productions: *The Einstein Project* (co-author Paul D'Andrea) off-Broadway and *Punch in America* (musical with Chris Jeffries), co-produced by Woolly Mammoth, Illusion Theatre and The Empty Space.

Shirley Lauro most recently premiered *A Piece of My Heart* at Actors Theatre of Louisville, which won The Kitteredge Award and Barbara Deming Prize, and was a finalist for the Susan Smith Blackburn Prize. More than 100 subsequent productions of *A Piece of My Heart* followed, including Manhattan Theatre Club, Stamford Theatre Works, International City Theatre, Bailiwick Repertory, a South African premiere which Lauro attended, sponsored by the U.S.I.A. and Natal Performing Arts Council. Other Actors Theatre premieres: *The Coal Diamond* (Heideman Award), *Nothing Immediate* and *Sunday Go to Meetin'*. Broadway: Tony-nominated *Open Admissions*, recipient of Dramatists Guild's Hull Warriner Award, *The New York Times* "10 Best Plays of the Year" list. *Open Admissions* was adapted by Lauro for a CBS Special starring Jane Alexander. Off-Broadway: *The Contest*. Latest play: *The Last Trial of Clarence Darrow*, EST Octoberfest 2000. Major fellowships: The Guggenheim, NEA, N.Y. Foundation for the Arts.

Craig Lucas is the author of plays (*Stranger*, *The Dying Gaul*, *God's Heart*, *Prelude to a Kiss*, *Blue Window*, *Reckless*, *Missing Persons*), movies (*Longtime Companion*, *Prelude to a Kiss*, *Reckless*, *Blue Window*), opera libretto (*Orpheus in Love*), musical books (*Three Postcards*, *Marry Me a Little*), and essays. He has received the Outer Critics Circle, Burns Mantle Best Musical, Drama-Logue, Obie, George and Elisabeth Marton, L.A. Drama Critics, GLAAD Media, Sundance Audience and Villager awards, as well as a Tony nomination and three Drama Desk nominations. He has been a Pulitzer finalist and is the recipient of Guggenheim, Rockefeller and NEA/TCG fellowships along with play commissions from South Coast Repertory, Hartford Stage and Actors Theatre of Louisville.

Eduardo Machado is the author of over 25 plays and several translations, including *Cuba and the Night, Stevie Wants to Play the Blues, A Burning Beach, Why to Refuse, Broken Eggs* and *When the Sea Drowns in Sand.* His plays have been produced in regional theaters all over the country, New York City and London. Some of these theaters include the Williamstown Theatre Festival, the Long Wharf Theater, the Mark Taper Forum, Actors Theatre of Louisville, the Ensemble Studio Theater, the American Place Theater, El Repertorio Español, the Los Angeles Theater Center and the New Mexico Repertory. Machado has recently completed writing and directing his first feature-length film, *Exiles in New York,* which premiered at the Santa Barbara Film Festival, AFI Film Festival, South by Southwest and Festival International Del Nuevo Cine Latino Americano. Machado is the head of Playwrighting at Columbia University and Co-Artistic Director at The Cherry Lane Theatre in New York.

Donald Margulies is a familiar name at Actors Theatre of Louisville, where two of his plays, *Dinner with Friends* and *July 7, 1994*, debuted at previous Humana Festivals. His plays include *Collected Stories* (Los Angeles Drama Critics' Circle Award, Pulitzer Prize finalist), *The Model Apartment* (Obie Award, Drama-Logue Award), *Sight Unseen* (Obie Award, Dramatists Guild/Hull-Warriner Award, Pulitzer Prize finalist, a Burns Mantle "Best Play"), *The Loman Family Picnic* (a Burns Mantle "Best Play"), *Found a Peanut, Pitching to the Star* and *What's Wrong With This Picture?* His adaptation of Sholem Asch's Yiddish classic, *God of Vengeance*, recently premiered at A Contemporary Theatre in Seattle. He was awarded the 2000 Pulitzer Prize for Drama for *Dinner with Friends*. He is a member of the council of The Dramatists Guild of America. Margulies lives with his wife and son in New Haven, Connecticut, where he teaches playwriting at Yale University.

Jane Martin returned to Actors Theatre with her latest play, *Anton in Show Business*, following her premiere of *Mr. Bundy* in the 22nd Humana Festival. Martin, a Kentuckian, first came to national attention for *Talking With*, a collection of monologues premiering in the 1982 Humana Festival. Since its New York premiere at the Manhattan Theatre Club in 1982, *Talking With* has been performed around the world, winning the Best Foreign Play of the Year award in Germany from *Theater Heute* magazine. Martin's *Keely and Du*, which premiered in the 1993 Humana Festival, was nominated for the Pulitzer Prize and won the American Theatre Critics Association Award for Best New Play in 1994. Her play *Jack and Jill* premiered in the 1996 Humana Festival and won the American Theatre Critics Association Award in 1997. Her other work includes *Middle-Aged White Guys* (1995 Humana Festival), *Cementville* (1991 Humana Festival) and *Vital Signs* (1990 Humana Festival). Martin's work has been translated into Spanish, French, German, Dutch, Russian and several other languages.

Susan Miller won her second Obie and the Susan Smith Blackburn Prize for her one-woman play, *My Left Breast*, which premiered at the Humana Festival. She has since performed it in theaters around the country. *Nasty Rumors and Final Remarks*, *Cross Country*, *Flux*, *For Dear Life*, *Confessions of a Female Disorder* and *It's Our Town, Too*, were produced by the Mark Taper Forum, O'Neill National Playwrights Conference, Second Stage, Trinity Repertory, Naked Angels and the Public Theater. She received the Publishing Triangle's Robert Chessley Lifetime Achievement Award in Playwriting. Miller, a Yaddo Fellow, has also received NEA and Rockefeller grants. She just completed a new play, *A Map of Doubt and Rescue*. She has written screenplays for Disney, Warner Bros., Universal and Fox 2000, among others.

John Olive's Actors Theatre of Louisville productions include *Clara's Play*, *Killers* and *Evelyn and the Polka King*. Other plays include *Standing on My Knees*, *Minnesota Moon*, *The Voice of the Prairie* and *The Aspern Papers*. Olive's work has been widely produced. His most recent play, *The Summer Moon*, won a 1997 Kennedy Center Award for Drama, premiered in 1998 at A Contemporary Theatre in Seattle, and played in 1999 at South Coast Repertory. Olive has written screenplays and teleplays for Disney, Amblin Entertainment, MGM/UA and Lorimar, among others. He lives in Minneapolis with his wife Mary and their son Michael.

Tanya Palmer is a playwright and a dramaturg. Her plays include *My Family is a Foreign Country*, *Nauvoo*, *Alone* and *Fatherland*. *Alone* was workshopped at Here Theatre in NYC and the Wilton Project in L.A., and was later produced at the Montreal Fringe Festival. *Fatherland* was produced at The Hangar Theatre as part of the Drama League's New Directors project. A 10-minute play, *Body Talk*, was produced at ATL and later published in *American Voice*. A dual citizen of Canada and the United States, Palmer received an M.F.A. in playwriting from York University in Toronto and was recently appointed Literary Manager at Actors Theatre of Louisville.

David Rambo's play *God's Man in Texas* received its world premiere at the 1999 Humana Festival, followed by productions at the Warehouse Theatre, Hippodrome, Florida Stage, Northlight Theatre, Stages Repertory and the Old Globe. Other plays include *Speaky-Spikey-Spokey*, presented at the Ashland New Plays Festival in Oregon, where he has been playwright-in-residence for the last three years—and a farce, *There's No Place Like House*, which enjoyed a long run in Los Angeles. Rambo is the author of several screenplays and freelances theatre journalism. He is a member of The Dramatists Guild.

Edwin Sánchez's notable productions include *Icarus*, produced by Actors Theatre of Louisville as part of the Humana Festival and by San Jose Repertory; *Barefoot Boy With Shoes On*, at Primary Stages in New York as part of their 1999-2000 season; and *Unmerciful Good Fortune* (AT&T On Stage New

Play Award, nominee Best New Play—Jeff Award), co-produced by Northlight Theatre and Victory Gardens Theater of Chicago. Other productions include *Clean* (Kennedy Center Fund for New American Plays winner), produced by Hartford Stage Company where it was nominated by the American Theater Critics Association for its annual New Play Award. Sanchez is a member of The Dramatists Guild and New Dramatists.

Adele Edling Shank has been at Actors Theatre of Louisville with *Sunset/Sunrise* (co-winner of the Great American Play Contest) and *Sand Castles*, two of her California Plays. Other full-length plays include *Winterplay*; *Stuck: A Freeway Comedy*; *The Grass House* and *Tumbleweed* (California Plays); *War Horses*; *Rocks in Her Pocket*; *With Allison's Eyes*; *The Wives of the Magi* (a play for December) and *Sex Slaves*. Recently, her play *Dry Smoke* was made into a chamber opera (music by Victor Kioulaphides) and her adaptation of *Stuck: A Freeway Comedy* was produced by Slovak Radio. Currently, she is working on a film adaptation of *With Allison's Eyes*. Shank has received numerous awards including Rockefeller and NEA Playwriting grants. She is head of playwriting at the University of California, San Diego and is an editor of *Theatre Forum* magazine.

Mayo Simon's plays have been produced in many theaters in the United States and Europe. These productions include *Walking to Waldheim* (Lincoln Center, New York), *L.A. Under Siege* (Mark Taper Forum), *A Rich Full Life* (Los Angeles Theatre Center), *These Men* (Magic Theatre, San Francisco), *Elaine's Daughter* (Actors Theatre of Louisville, Philadelphia Theatre Company), *The Old Lady's Guide to Survival* (Actors Theatre of Louisville, Pittsburgh Public Theater, Lambs Club Theater, New York), and *Split* (Aurora Theatre Company, Berkeley, California). Simon's plays have also been produced in England, Ireland, Germany, Norway, Sweden, Denmark and Italy. Many are published by Dramatic Publishing Company.

Val Smith is the author of numerous plays which have been published and produced nationally. Her first full-length drama, *The Gamblers*, won the Playhouse on the Square's Mid-South Playwright's Competition, and was produced at American Stage Theatre in New Jersey in 1992. Her second full-length, *Ain't We Got Fun*, was commissioned and produced by Actors Theatre of Louisville in the 1993 Classics in Context Festival—The Roaring Twenties. She is the recipient of awards from the Kentucky Women's Foundation and the Kentucky Arts Council. Her most recent full-length play, *Marguerite Bonet*, is published in *Best Plays by Women of 1998*. Her 10-minute play *Meow* premiered at the 1998 Humana Festival.

DIRECTOR'S NOTES

DIRECTOR'S NOTES

DIRECTOR'S NOTES

DIRECTOR'S NOTES

DIRECTOR'S NOTES

DIRECTOR'S NOTES